ETA COHEN VIOLIN METHOD
Book 1
Teacher's book
with violin duet part and notes

The violin duet part is also available in a separate volume containing piano accompaniments by Richard Drakeford

PAXTON

Cat. No. 91 6175

Book 1 of the Eta Cohen Violin Method is available in three volumes:
    Violin part with teacher's notes   Cat. No. 91 6136 08
    Piano accompaniments   Cat. No. 91 6137 06
    Teacher's book with violin duet part and notes   Cat. No. 91 6175

The violin duet parts by Richard Drakeford are intended as an *alternative* to the piano accompaniments. They differ from the piano parts in many respects and thus cannot be used with the piano.

Also available:

Eta Cohen Violin Method Book 2
    Violin part   Cat. No. 91 6170
    Piano accompaniments with violin duet part   Cat. No. 91 6171

Eta Cohen Violin Method Book 3
    Pupil's book (violin)   Cat. No. 91 6172
    Piano accompaniment book with violin duet part   Cat. No. 91 6173
    Teacher's book (violin duet part)   Cat. No. 91 6174

Learning to Play the Violin:
    3 Cassettes for use with the Eta Cohen Violin Method Book 1
                                                            Cat. Nos. 91 6167 08 01
                                                                      91 6167 08 02
                                                                      91 6167 08 03

CONTENTS OF BOOK 1

(Violin Duet parts by Richard Drakeford are indicated with an asterisk*)

The page numbers refer to this volume (Teacher's book)

FOREWORD

In this revised edition of the *First-Year Violin Method*, now renamed the *Eta Cohen Violin Method*, Book 1, my main purpose has been to make the book easier to follow by the addition of more instructions and detailed photographs.

A few of the tunes used in the earlier edition have been omitted because they were either unsuitable or too difficult. Some will reappear in the revised edition of the *Second-Year Violin Method*, similarly renamed. However, in order to make this book more suitable for very young children a number of easy exercises have been added.

The Method can be used for private or class tuition with children of all ages, as well as adult beginners, and I would give the following advice to teachers as the most effective way of using this book.

Rate of progress

Teach one point at a time and do not move forward until the work at each stage has been thoroughly assimilated and understood. The teacher should remember that if the pupil moves very slowly at the beginning he will always make more rapid progress at the next stage.

The book is divided into 30 'steps'. There is no inflexible rule about the speed at which pupils should progress – this varies according to their ability and the size of class. Although each step may take anything from one to four weeks (or even longer) to complete, it is inadvisable to cover more than one step per lesson: every step introduces something new and it is always best to allow time for the proper absorption of new work or ideas.

Which String?

It is best to start with one string – the D string – and then use only the D and A strings for some time. Good tone is easier to achieve on these two, and difficulties of tuning and reading are minimized. Encourage pupils to sing the music; this is easiest within the compass of D – D'.

Position

Begin with pizzicato playing, holding the violin in banjo position. This enables the pupil to play the first simple pieces without having to cope with the initial strain of the difficult violin-hold. He soon moves on to pizzicato with the violin under the chin – just a little at first – increasing the time gradually. When the techniques of left and right hands have been well learned separately, the co-ordination of the two hands will be comparatively painless. As bowing becomes more proficient, pizzicato playing can be dropped gradually.

Bowing

After the first few lessons introduce the bow-hold and then attempt easy bowing exercises. Proceed very gradually, first practising away from the violin, then on the D string using only the top half of the bow (middle to point), and then on to the A string but always keeping the bow moving at the same speed.

Next, teach playing from heel to middle of the bow and, finally, join the two half bows into whole bows.

For some time use only half or whole bows, with a constant bow speed, until the pupil is accustomed to using every inch of the hair. Only when this is achieved should he go on to the next stage – playing with various lengths and speeds of bow.

There are many bowing marks throughout the book, so that if a pupil stops in the middle of a piece he can carry on using the correct up or down bow without having to go back to the beginning of a bar or line. He should always be encouraged to pick up immediately at any point in the music indicated by the teacher.

Dynamics

It is rather difficult to know when to introduce dynamics. From the beginning encourage pupils to play with firm, strong tone near the bridge. Later, show them how to play softly, away from the bridge, and gradually introduce various shades of tone in between. The teacher could introduce some tonal variety from Step 19 onwards, but it may be some time before pupils can accomplish this successfully. The main objective should be to achieve a good sound by insisting on correct bowing technique and training pupils to *listen*, for tone *quality* as well as for correct intonation.

ETA COHEN

SUMMARY OF THE METHOD

Page Step (in Pupil's book)		Rhythm Exercises	Exercises in banjo position	Exercises in under chin position (pizz.)	Bowing
4	1	Ex. 1—crotchets only on D	Learning banjo position for playing open strings		
6	2	Ex. 2—crotchets and minims on D	Learning banjo position for playing with fingers		
7	3		Exs. 3, 4, 5—D E F♯	Learning to hold violin under chin	
8	4	Ex. 10—crotchets and minims on D and A	Exs. 6, 7, 8, 9—D E F♯ G	Revision of Exs. 3, 4, 5	
9	5		Exs. 11, 12, 13, 14—D E F♯ G A	Revision of Exs. 6, 7	
10	6		Ex. 15—D E F♯ G A B	Revision of Exs. 8, 9	Learning the bow-hold
11	7		Exs. 16, 17—D E F♯ G A B	Revision of Exs. 11, 12, 13	Bowing silently without violin
12	8		Ex. 18—D E F♯ G A B	Revision of Exs. 14, 15	Bowing on open D string, middle to point
13	9		Exs. 20, 21, 22—notes of complete scale of D major	Revision of Exs. 16, 17, 18	Bowing exercises 19 (a), (b), (c) on open D string—minims only, middle to point
14	10		No more banjo playing	Revision of Exs. 20, 21, 22. Exs. 23, 24, 25 only under chin	Exs. 4, 5—bowing with fingers—minims only, middle to point
15	11	Ex. 26—dotted minims		Exs. 27, 28, 29 only under chin	Exs. 6, 7, 8, 9—bowing with fingers—minims only, middle to point
16	12			No more pizzicato pieces. The rest can be played pizz. when desired	Exs. 30, 14, 20—exercises for changing from D to A string—minims only, middle to point
16	13				Exs. 19, 30, 4, 5, 6, 7, 8, 9, 14, 20—minims only, from heel to middle
17	14	Ex. 33—a scale in semibreves			Exs. 31, 32, 33, 34, 35—how to join half bows and play semibreves with whole bows
18	15				Revision of Exs. 6, 7, 8, 9, 14, 20—with whole bows. Exs. 36, 37, 38, 39—minims with whole bows
19	16				Ex. 40 and revision of Exs. 11, 12, 13, 15, 16, 17, 18, 21, 22, 23, 24, 25—minims with whole bows, crotchets with half bows at heel or point
19	17				Exs. 41, 42—whole bows for crotchets, slower bows for minims—dotted minims and semibreves. Revision of Exs. 27, 28, 29 using WBS
20	18	Ex. 43—quavers			Exs. 44, 45, 46,—whole bows for crotchets, slow whole bows for minims, short bows for quavers
21	19	Ex. 48—a piece in $\frac{2}{4}$ time			Exs. 47, 48, 49—bows getting gradually quicker and shorter—bowing on E string. Dynamics introduced
22	20				Exs. 50, 51, 52, 53—as Step 19
23	21				Exs. 54, 55, 56, 57—slurs. Ex. 58—fourth finger
24	22				Exs. 59, 60, 61—broken slurs. Revision of Ex. 54
25	23				Exs. 62, 63, 64—pieces combining various types of bowing
26	24	Ex. 65—dotted crotchets			Exs. 66, 67—as Step 23
27	25				Exs. 68, 69, 70, 71—bowing on G string. Ex. 72—exercise in double stopping
28	26				Ex. 73—double stopping. Ex. 74—broken slurs. Ex. 75—exercise at heel of bow
29	27				Ex. 76—exercise at point or middle of bow. Ex. 77, 78—various types of bowing
30	28				Exs. 79, 80, 81—various types of bowing
31	29				Exs. 82, 83, 84—various types of bowing
32	30	Exs. 85, 86—$\frac{6}{8}$ time			Exs. 87, 88—pieces in $\frac{6}{8}$ time

If a teacher should prefer to start with bowing instead of pizzicato, he could omit the two columns marked 'Exercises in banjo position' and 'Exercises in under chin position'. Similarly, a teacher preferring to start with pizz. under chin could omit the column marked 'Exercises in banjo position'.

ABBREVIATIONS AND MUSICAL TERMS
STEP 1

♩ crotchet – 1 beat

♩ minim – 2 beats

♩. dotted minim – 3 beats

○ semibreve – 4 beats

♫ 2 quavers – 2 half beats

♩. dotted crotchet – 1½ beats

𝄽 crotchet rest

𝄾 quaver rest

minim rest

1 bar rest

2 bars rest

$\frac{4}{4}$ 4 crotchets in a bar

$\frac{3}{4}$ 3 crotchets in a bar

$\frac{2}{4}$ 2 crotchets in a bar

$\frac{6}{8}$ 6 quavers in a bar

⊓ down bow

V up bow

Pt point of bow

M middle of bow

H heel of bow

WB whole bow

⌒ slur

⌢ broken slur

arco with the bow

pizz. pizzicato (plucked)

0 open string

1 first finger

2 second finger

3 third finger

4 fourth finger

1—— keep finger down

p piano – soft

f forte – loud

mp mezzo piano – fairly soft

mf mezzo forte – fairly loud

dim. diminuendo – gradually softer

cresc. crescendo – gradually louder

⌒ a pause

rall. gradually slower

‖: :‖ repeat the music between the signs

[1 first time bar

[2 second time bar

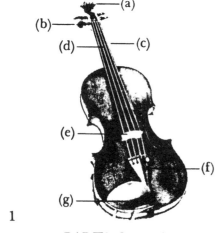

1

PARTS OF VIOLIN

(a) scroll (b) pegs (c) neck
(d) fingerboard (e) bridge
(f) tailpiece (g) chin rest
There are four strings starting from the right E A D G.

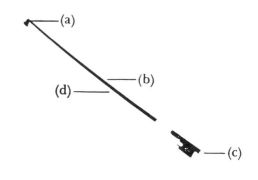

2

PARTS OF BOW

(a) point (b) middle
(c) heel or nut (d) hair
Put bow back into your case until you need it (Step 6).

TUNING

(You will only use the D string at first, so tune it at the beginning of each practice. Keep checking to see if it needs retuning.)

(a) Hold violin upright on knee, left hand round neck, left thumb free for plucking.

(b) Keep *perfect silence* and *listen* to the note D being played. (When practising at home ask someone else to play the note on the piano).

(c) After D has been played a second time, *hum* the note.

(d) After a moment's pause, hum it again, to see if you can remember the sound. Be sure that you have the exact pitch in your head.

(e) If you use an adjuster pluck the D string with the left thumb and turn the adjuster with the right hand.

At the same time, listen carefully, while the teacher continues to play the note. If you use the peg for tuning, turn it very slowly with the left hand, and pluck with the right thumb – away from you if the string is flat and towards you if sharp, pressing the peg firmly into the hole all the time while continuing to pluck the string with the right thumb until the string is in tune.

RHYTHM EXERCISES ON D STRING PLAYED PIZZICATO [plucked]

STEP 2

RHYTHM EXERCISES ON D STRING [pizzicato]

STEP 3

FINGER EXERCISES ON D STRING

STEP 4
FINGER EXERCISES ON D STRING

Simple Alternative Version

8

First Version

9(a)

13

RHYTHM EXERCISE ON D AND A STRINGS

10

TEACHER

4

7

STEP 5
BELLS
Ostinato

STEP 6

HASLEMERE

Anonymous

TWINKLE, TWINKLE, LITTLE STAR

Traditional Nursery Rhyme

BLOWING BUBBLES

Polish Folk Song

STEP 9

BOWING EXERCISES ON THE D STRING

19(a)

TEACHER

Goosey, goosey gander

(b)

Tom, Tom, the Piper's Son

(c)

19 *Goosey, goosey gander*

23

STEP 10

CULBACH
First Version

J. Scheffler, *Heilge Seelenlust*, 1657

24(a) Smoothly and flowing

pizz.

TEACHER

mp

mp

6

STEP 11

TALLIS' ORDINAL

Thomas Tallis

27 Smoothly with expression

pizz.

TEACHER

arco

p

arco

p

(*)

6

mp

p

p

STEP 12
BOWING EXERCISE FOR CHANGING STRINGS

STEP 14
EXERCISES FOR WHOLE BOWS

35

TEACHER

Little Brown Jug

7

13

STEP 15
DOWN THE STEPS

38

Smoothly and firmly

TEACHER

7

13

ON THE SWING

39

STEP 17

CRADLE SONG

First Version

German Folk Song

41(a)

QUEEN MARY

Scottish Folk Song

STEP 19

FRERE JACQUES

A Round

French Folk Song

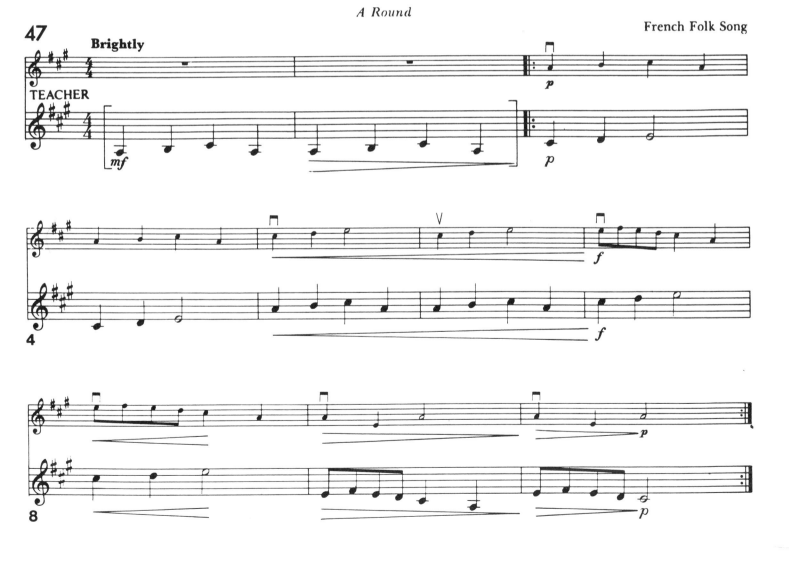

STEP 21
THE VICAR OF BRAY

English Song, 17th century

WINTER GOODBYE

German Song

STEP 23
CHERRY RIPE

C. E. Horn

STEP 24

HERE'S A HEALTH UNTO HIS MAJESTY

English Song, 1667

STEP 27

PETER PIPER

Traditional Nursery Rhyme

Melody reprinted from *The Oxford Nursery Song Book* by permission of Oxford University Press.

STEP 30

RHYTHM EXERCISES

85(a)

86

String Music for the Student

Violin

Eta Cohen	Violin Method Book 1
	Book 2
	Book 3
Richard Rodney Bennett	Up Bow, Down Bow *(violin)*
Robert Jacoby	Violin Technique
Michael Rose	Fiddler's Ten
David Stone	Eight Pieces in the Third Position
Scales and Arpeggios	

Viola

Richard Rodney Bennett	Up Bow, Down Bow *(viola)*
Una Bolitho	Ten Carols
Alison Milne	Playing the Viola
Scales and Arpeggios	

Cello

Benoy and Burrowes	Cello Method First Year
	Second Year
	Third Year
Burrowes, arr.	Six Easy Pieces *(solo or duet)*
Cole and Shuttleworth	Playing the Cello *(tutor)*
Evans	Cello Time
Maurice Eisenberg	Cello Playing of Today *(tutor)*
Scales and Arpeggios	

Double Bass

Colin Evans	Basic Bass *(open strings only)*